LEADERSHIP BY STORYTELLING

The Best Way to Learn
Good Leadership Principles

**Have fun. Work hard. Play hard
Do these with your team.**

By Dr. Tom DePaoli
Illustrated by Laurie Barrows

Text © 2019 by Dr. Tom DePaoli

Contact the author at
www.apollosolutions.us or
www.drtombooks.com

Illustrations© 2019 Laurie Barrows
www.lauriebarrows.com

ISBN-13: ISBN: 9781091175754

Printed in the United States of America

Published in the United States of America

Introduction

The purpose of this book is to provide some excellent principles of good leadership. The principles are illustrated with stories that reinforce the principles. One of the oldest methods of passing down knowledge is oral storytelling. Usually an ancient sage would be the keeper of the stories and pass them down to other tribe members. I also recommend this method for leaders.

Here are some advantages of storytelling:

The brain stores information by stories.

Stories are humanizing and stimulate creativity.

Storytelling improves listening skills.

Storytelling builds a team culture.

It encourages collaboration.

First, creating the right atmosphere and teamwork is essential in order to establish the validity of this method. The trust of all members of the team and non-attribution is essential. The leader of the team should lead off and share personal leadership stories of success and failures. There should be a general framework for the stories. In the framework, structure the stories to first give a background of the situation or issue, then tell how resources are gathered to address the issue (approach), and finally reveal the results. Often the approach to solving the problem is more important than the actual results. Colleagues or followers should be encouraged to ask questions and to suggest more appropriate approaches. Leaders have many touch points or people involved throughout work experiences.

I have provided illustrations to help clarify the principles and the stories. I urge the reader to gather leadership stories to share with fellow leaders and followers. I believe the growth in leadership abilities will be much stronger via the use of leadership stories.

"I hope that you enjoy the book.", Dr. Tom

TABLE of CONTENTS

Never lie to your followers or your superiors. Keep your word always.   **1**

Listen to your followers' problems and help them.   **2**

Don't believe what you hear from the media or so-called experts. Be skeptical. **4**

Stand up for what you believe in. Do not be silent to idiots or insanity.   **6**

Never neglect details. Walk the process. Do it yourself to learn how to do it.   **8**

On many things do not ask permission ask for forgiveness. Always try to make things better. Show initiative.   **11**

This is not a perfect world, so there are many opportunities to improve. So, improve.   **13**

Hire the best people, get people who are better and smarter than you.   **16**

Encourage people to always improve their skills. Lead by example here.   **17**

Don't chase the latest management fads. The situation usually dictates which approach best accomplishes the team's mission.   **19**

Be positive always, but do not sugar coat a crisis.   21

Look for people with integrity and intelligence and who care about and help others.   23

Offer solutions, not problems and try to keep the solutions simple.   24

Go with your gut if you do not have enough data. Avoid data paralysis.   26

Always trust the people in the field, closer to the work or on the shop floor more.   28

Have fun, work hard and play hard. Do these with your team.   30

Leadership is lonely but accept the blame as it arrives on your desk.   32

Leadership is the art of accomplishing the impossible, so what if no one has ever done it before. Do it.   33

Share your hard lessons learned with others. Do not embellish them.   36

Be humble but be confident.   39

Praise people who do a good job often.   40

Treat people like you would like to be treated.   42

Work hard and volunteer for the tough assignments.   44

Be pleasant, positive and polite.   47

Always do your best even for the tasks that you hate to do.   50

Take an interest in people, not toys, technology or hardware.   51

About the Author   53

Summaries of the Author's Other Books   55

About the Illustrator   77

Notes & Ideas   78

Never Lie To Your Followers Or Your Superiors. Keep Your Word Always.

I was once a department head in production center with twelve people reporting to me. At a meeting of department heads we were informed that there would be a 10% downsizing across all department within this budget year. The criteria in each department would be that last three performance reviews. The employees with the worst reviews would be downsized. I was the only one who asked how the company was going to help the employees downsized. Human Resources did have a response. Downsized employees would get severance pay based on their longevity, six months of health care and outplacement help. After the meeting, rumors spread throughout the company like wildfire. I decided to hold a department meeting and clarify what was going to happen with my employees. I openly revealed everything I knew about the downsizing at the meeting. When people asked, I told them I could not promise that they would retain, or lose their job, that was to be decided. Never lie to your followers or your superiors. Keep your word always.

Listen To Your Followers' Problems And Help Them

I once had an employee who was initially very upset that I took over as leader of the department. She thought that she deserved to be promoted and become the leader. She had more experience than me. She was very cold to me and resisted any initiatives that I proposed. Shortly thereafter, her mother became very sick and it got to the point that she needed caregivers. I gave her as much time of as I could and was very flexible with her work duties and responsibilities. She finally requested family leave for eight weeks and it was granted. While she was gone, I attempted to do as much of her work as possible and got a very good understanding of her duties, systems and techniques. I stayed late many nights and weekends working at both my job and hers.

When she came back from family leave, she expected piles of work awaiting her and very hectic weeks. She was surprised that I had kept up and completed almost all of the work. She came into my office and started to cry and I thought that something had happened to her mother. Instead she was grateful for what I had done and thanked me informing me that no boss had ever done anything so kind. I then suggested that we make a request to our information technology department to upgrade some for the systems that she used, and I was now familiar with by doing her job. We jointly filled out the request that day and it was installed in three weeks.

Her attitude towards me completely turned around. Whenever there was a tough project, she volunteered for it. She became the most loyal employee to me in the department and a friend. As a leader, if someone has a problem and needs help, especially when it is personal or family related, go out of your way to help them. Listen to your followers' problems and help them.

Don't Believe What You Hear From The Media Or So-Called Experts. Be Skeptical.

A major company that I worked for wanted to redesign their internal website. They assigned their best programmers and some marketing people to design the new website. They hired a team of website design experts to advise them. The experts showed the company the latest media ratings of websites and their effectiveness. The programmers then insisted on putting all the latest bells and whistles on the website as advised by the website experts. They soon convinced the project leader that these were necessary upgrades. Unfortunately, they did not complete any voice of the customer exercises in the design of the web-site; they did not do any surveys or focus groups. They did not figure out what was critical to the actual internal website customers. They were too enamored with the latest website designs and what the experts told them to do.

The first preview or showing of the new website to customers was a disaster that ended in chaos. The programmers were disheartened and did not know what to do. A senior manager suggested some voice of the customer tools to the team, and they quickly started them. Small internal customer focus groups yielded the best information. They gradually redesigned the website and incorporated many of the suggestions of the customers. The website was a huge success and many of its principles were reapplied to the company's other external customer websites, but not without thoroughly testing the voice of the website customers first. Don't believe what you hear from the media or so-called experts be skeptical.

Stand Up For What You Believe In. Do Not Be Silent To Idiots Or Insanity.

When I was working for a large chemical company, I was told to run the numbers to justify an inventory project that would write down inventory and put in place a new inventory software system. I ran the numbers many different ways and presented the best results that I could that were based on accepted accounting and inventory practices. My justification was subsequently presented to my vice-president. He called me up and told me to fudge or inflate the numbers so that the capital committee would approve the project. I told him that I could not inflate the numbers and use unaccepted practices to justify the project. I remarked that that would be dishonest and misleading. I also noted that we would lose all credibility especially if we wanted future projects. He went on a vicious rant and informed me that he was the expert on projects not me. The project was not proposed that year.

Next year after the budget was approved, I was called into my boss's office. He informed me that my position was not in next year's budget and my position was being eliminated. Off the record, he was honest enough to tell me that the vice-president was responsible for the decision and that the vice president was personally going to re-propose the inventory project in the new budget year. Fortunately, two weeks later I landed another position that was a step advancement that paid me 40% more salary. Stand up for what you believe in. Do not be silent to idiots or insanity.

Never Neglect Details. Walk The Process. Do It Yourself To Learn How To Do It.

I had just reported into a new organization and was given a huge orientation packet with a three-page checklist. When I asked individuals how long it would take to complete the check-in process the answers varied from 4 hours to two weeks. There were four different types of employee groups but just one check-in process and a single type check list. Each new person had a sponsor. I asked my sponsor if I had to complete all of the checklist items and he replied yes, I did. There happened to be another new employee reporting on the same day as I did, so we decided to partner up and do the check-in together. Both of us inquired about certain aspects of the check-in and orientation process and soon discovered that we got different and wildly different answers on the check-in process.

As a Lean Six Sigma Black Belt I decided to document the check-in process along with my partner and record data on the actual process. We started off both with clipboards and I actually used my smartphone's pedometer to record our steps and the time spent at each check-in station. We soon discovered that often the person who was supposed to check us in was not present to perform the check-in. We had to then come back when they were present. There was no coordination between check-in spots and much of the check-in requirements were rather unnecessary. Often a department head would just initial our check-in sheet. Some would just hand us documents to read later and sign the sheet. Some would update their databases so we asked to watch them do this process and we observed.

Bottom line by walking the process we found out how inefficient it was, and soon determined what stops were actually value adding or useful. Much of the check-in process was only relevant to a particular employee group (the organization had four of them). We both completed the check-in process in seven business days and presented our check-in sheets to our boss.

We had at least an hour discussion with him about the process and recommended forming a kaizen team, which would have members from all four employee groups, to try and improve the process. He agreed to our suggestion and both me and my partner were appointed Kaizen co-leaders. We had instant credibility with the team because we had just actually walked and completed the check-in process recently. After two weeks of work with the team and other team members walking the check-in process again, we reduced the check-in time to two business days or less for each employee group. In a year after putting much of the check-in process online we reduced it to one business day. More importantly from a morale and first impression aspect to a new employee the organization appeared well organized and competent. Never neglect details. Walk the process. Do it yourself to learn how to do it.

On Many Things Do Not Ask Permission Ask For Forgiveness Always Try To Make Things Better Show Initiative

I and a colleague were software installers on a major e-commerce software system that was to be installed at a large multinational company. The software was somewhat specific to each plant or service department but over 80% was the same. Teams of consultants would visit each plant and try to gather the necessary data that the software installers needed to install the software. That data was then given to the software installer to use to install the e-commerce software. The error rate for the new plant systems was atrocious and the punch lists (errors) were huge. The client was growing increasingly skeptical about the software and was threatening to cancel the contract.

The installation data was provided on spreadsheets, handwritten papers, MS Word documents, etc. There was no order or structure to how the data was collected. When the software installers received the data, it was almost impossible to be accurate with the data. Much time was wasted calling the consultants trying to verify the data. The software installers took a bold step without corporate buy-in.

The installers noted that there were 420 different screens that data had to be entered on when the software was installed. They brainstormed what to do and came up with a plan to design an Excel spreadsheet with 420 corresponding sheets, or one for each screen. Essentially, each spreadsheet closely mimicked the entry screen with instructions about the data. Similar data was linked to certain spreadsheets to avoid duplicate and redundant data entry. The spreadsheet soon became more and more sophisticated and made the data collector's job much easier by eliminating duplicate entries and using creative macros.

The data entry error rate dropped from over 50 percent to less than 1 percent. The client's confidence in the new e-commerce system rose and they ordered more multiple new installations. On many things do not ask permission ask for forgiveness. Always try to make things better and show initiative.

This Is Not A Perfect World, So There Are Many Opportunities To Improve. So, Improve.

In the Navy Reserve I once had a boss (leader) who just disliked me and was not shy about reminding me that he disliked me. He also bragged in advance that he was going to give me a poor performance review. Obviously, this was very discouraging, but instead of wallowing in the unfair situation and acting like a victim, I developed a strategy. I gathered information on possible projects or opportunities that I could correct or improve. Many of them had been neglected for years. I decided to identify and complete three projects that no one had ever done before in the history of the Navy Reserve. The improvements I discovered could be tracked with metrics and monitored. These were very tough and time-consuming projects, but I completed them before my performance review.

For the performance review an individual is always asked to submit their accomplishments. So, I submitted the three projects. At first, my boss did not want to include them, but I said that I would exercise my right to add a supplement to my performance review, that would include the projects. He relented and included the projects in my performance review. The word of me completing these projects soon spread across the entire command and other parts of the Navy Reserve. My boss did write the performance review but his less than stellar words about me just did not match or align with the accomplishments of the ground-breaking projects.

An Admiral then invited me to speak at his conference. Later by luck, the same Admiral was appointed the head of the promotion board that promoted me to Captain. I like to think that my presentation on the project helped clarify his judgement about me. When you get a bad leader, never let it discourage you from doing your very best. This is not a perfect world, so there are many opportunities to improve, so improve.

Hire The Best People. Get People Who Are Better And Smarter Than You.

We had an opening in our department for a mid-level supplier engineer position. When we interviewed for the job, we had an outstanding candidate. The candidate had a masters in mechanical engineering and was working on their PhD. During the team interview, it was obvious that he was very smart and prepared. He stated the company vision and mission statement from memory and excerpts from the annual report. I wanted to hire him on the spot but Human Resources insisted on a background check.

We hired him for the job, and he as a great fit. Two months later the company opened up a small satellite facility nearby to run a new product line. They wanted a full-time supplier engineer at the facility. The deadlines and production pressures were to be immense. I sat down with the newly hired supplier engineer, and found out that he had actually did some research on the technology being used in the startup. I asked him if he was interested, and he stated that he was happy to be considered. He started at the satellite facility the next day and the startup was an immense success. Hire the best people. Get people who are better and smarter than you

Encourage People To Always Improve Their Skills. Lead By Example Here.

I have seven professional certifications and a PhD. I always encouraged my employees to pursue more training and to improve their skills. I have conducted pre-certification training and always celebrated when one of my employees achieved a certification or a degree. Part of this drive to get better comes from the fact that at least four times in my life I was thrown into or promoted into a position that I knew absolutely nothing about. My only recourse was to learn as fast as I could and get help from the professional organization relevant to my position. My employees would notice me staying after work and studying for a particular course or certification. More importantly, I fought for reimbursement for them when they pursed additional training. Encourage people to always improve their skills. Lead by example here.

Don't Chase The Latest Management Fads. The Situation Usually Dictates Which Approach Dictates Which Approach Best Accomplishes The Team's Mission.

I was hired as a lean six sigma consultant for a large transportation organization. The organization had a history of trying the latest management fads, business book of the month and other short-term trends. I met with many company employees and it was obvious that they were very skeptical and had seen many management vogues or initiatives tried and dropped quickly. The culture was such that they did not have much patience with projects that did not get relatively quick results.

I soon realized that I had to change my approach and assume a more situational leadership style. I knew that a typical full-blown lean six sigma project normally took six months and was very tedious. I decided to adjust my approach and start with kaizens which were a quicker form of lean six sigma projects and only lasted two weeks or less. The first kaizen only lasted three days. I had front loaded much of the work to myself ahead of time which significantly shortened the project sessions.

We kept to kaizens only for over a year and then tried a six month lean six sigma project after our string of kaizen success. Don't chase the latest management fads. The situation usually dictates which approach dictates which approach best accomplishes the team's mission.

Be Positive Always But Do Not Sugar Coat A Crisis

When I took over as a new Employee Relations Manager there was a backlog of over a thousand unanswered grievances. The Employee Relations Manager position had been vacant for over six months and the grievances were not answered. No one had taken any initiative of answering the grievances. The atmosphere in the plant was hostile to say the least. The process for answering grievances and the stages was very well documented and clear. There were three stages to the process. The grievances had not even been answered at the first stage. Contractually you could not change the process unless the union agreed to the change.

There were two administrative assistants that I had reporting to me. They were visibly upset and overwhelmed. We soon realized that the union just wanted the grievances answered. I remained positive and told them that I was sure that we could get through the grievances and answer them quickly. They were skeptical. I did tell them that we were under the gun or in a crisis mode. The union might file an unfair labor practices complaint against us if we did not get to work and answer the backlog of grievances.

We then decided to use an affinity-type tool often used in understanding the voice of the customer. We started to classify the grievances by type and soon discovered that generally there were only seven categories or types of grievances. Then with the help of a database that I set up, we entered all the grievances and sorted them by the agreed-to seven affinity types. We proceeded to craft similar but consistent answers to the grievances by affinity type and moved the all grievances out of the first step. The database gave us an advantage of answering the grievances consistently and quickly. We now had a history of our answers for future grievances.

The union was astounded that we had answered all the grievances, although many were not the answers that they wanted; they now had answers that they could show to their union members. We had introduced a professional way to track and answer future grievances. Be positive always but do not sugar coat a crisis

Look For People With Integrity And Intelligence And Who Care About And Help Others

When we interviewed people for employment, we used behavior-based questions and many other questions. We also asked every candidate what they did to give back to society. This usually demonstrated how they cared about people and society. It also demonstrated a focus not on just themselves but on others. We did weigh this heavily in our selection process. Look for people with Integrity and intelligence and who care about and help others.

Offer Solutions, Not Problems And Try To Keep The Solutions Simple.

My team was sent overseas to work in a warehouse in a third world country and assist in inventory verification and the shipping of items to another location. When we started one of the forklift operators got on a forklift and started to work. The brakes were not working properly and luckily the forklift did not crash. My deputy was aghast and near panic. He came to me with the problem and asked what to do next. I decided that it was time to instruct my deputy in offering solutions to problems not just stating the problem. I suggested composing a forklift safety checklist for the forklift driver before they start the shift and just to be safe have two individuals complete the checklist and sign it when it is completed. He soon caught on and then used initiative and contacted the forklift manufacturer to provide their checklist before the forklift was operated. The manufacturer also sent us a video on how to check their forklifts before operation. My deputy then used this solutions approach for the rest of the trip. Offer solutions, not problems and try to keep the solutions simple.

Go With Your Gut If You Do Not Have Enough Data. Avoid Data Paralysis.

One of the companies I worked for was undergoing a rapid growth spurt. Sales increased 500% in one year. All the internal systems and processes were experiencing severe growing pains. Warehouse space was at a premium for both finished and unfinished product. An internal plant space utilization team was formed to deal with the need for more space. Everyone on the team had different ideas for maximizing the square footage of the warehouse but most of it was in a two-dimensional mode or length x width of the storage. I knew from my industrial engineering background that volume or length x width x height had to be considered. Most of the storage utilization data we had was old and inaccurate. It was hard to get a handle on the data. We were under tremendous pressure to get solutions.

One of the major materials that we stored was large corrugated cases or what we called knockdowns. They took up over 50% of our storage space. They were stacked in bundles of 100 three high (300 total). I was curious as to why this was done and asked the forklift drivers if they knew why. They said that that previous materials manager required the bundles to be in 100s, because it made it easier for him to take inventory. This piqued my curiosity and I called our corrugated case or knockdown supplier. They remarked that we were the only customer that required a bundle count of 100. I did not wait for a study or more data; I went with my gut and told them to increase the bundle count to 150 from 100.

The forklift drivers proceeded to stack these 150 count bundles three high also. There were no stability issues. Thus, in the same square footage, we went from 300 corrugated cases to 450 corrugated cases. This was a storage space utilization increase of plus 50% at no cost. This greatly decreased the amount of new warehouse needed to support the sales growth spurt. Go with your gut if you do not have enough data. Avoid data paralysis.

Always Trust The People In The Field Closer To The Work, Not Staff.

A headquarters of a large organization had some issues with certain inventory discrepancies. They developed a new report for the field to help correct the variabilities. The report design and requirements were developed by staff experts and clerks. I was asked to go to various field sites and show the workers the report, explain why it was being proposed and ask them for their opinion of the report. The workers in the field just exploded in criticism of the report, ripping it and mocking it in no uncertain terms. They laughed at the design and methods used in the report. They remarked that most workers would either ignore or "gun deck" or fake the report. I knew that I could not go back to headquarters with just criticism of the report and complaints. I decided to stay a few extra days and with a group of workers and redesign the report and make some suggestions.

When I returned to headquarters the staff was disappointed with the reaction, but once I showed them the suggested modification by the workers, most admitted that the field's design and suggestions were better. They were incorporated in the newly designed report and it was well received in the field. Always trust the people in the field closer to the work, not staff.

Have Fun Work Hard Play Hard. Do These With Your Team.

As a leader or boss, I always thought it was important to do fun activities together as a team. Some of the activities included picnics, volleyball games, shopping trips, dinners, attending sporting events, and other group events. One of my teams had worked long and hard putting in a new Enterprise Resource Planning software system and getting all the modifications right. I let them pick the celebration activity. The team voted to go to a golf jamboree together as a team. All of us won some prize for various degrees of golf skill or golf ineptitude and we enjoyed a great dinner at the country club restaurant. At the dinner they could not resist taking shots at my not so great golf skills so they presented me with an award. It was a cheap compass. They remarked that where I usually hit a golf ball, so deep in the rough, I would need a compass to get back to the fairway. It did get the biggest laughs. Have fun, work hard. Do these with your team.

Leadership Is Lonely But Accept The Blame As It Arrives On Your Desk.

I was the leader of a purchasing department that had just sent out bids for a major project worth millions of dollars. We had decided on the supplier to accept and were going to contact them One of my buyers was to fax the acceptance to the winning supplier along with their entire bid package. The buyer made a mistake when faxing the acceptance and the acceptance and winning bid package went out to all the bidding suppliers (a group fax transmission).

I immediately called all the bidding suppliers and apologized for "my" mistake. I took the blame for the errant faxes myself and assured them that it would not happen again. I personally met with the supplier who won the bid and asked if they now had any concerns now that their competitors had seen their bid. Fortunately, nothing secret or revealing was in the bid. Leadership is lonely but accept the blame as it arrives on your desk

Leadership Is The Art Of Accomplishing The Impossible. So, What Is No One Has Ever Done It Before.

I worked for a large company that had a large plant. The plant was separated by a major state highway that split the production areas from the distribution warehouse area. The company had put an enclosed tube with a case conveyor over the highway connecting the two highway divided facilities. The cases would right through the tube into the distribution center. The company was expanding and room was needed for two major production lines and more storage space.

At first the company went to their local state representative asking for permission for the state to consider closing the highway and rerouting traffic. The plan was to put a new complete building the highway and add more production lines and storage space. Both buildings would now be connected to a new building in the middle. The state representative objected and cited all sorts of hurdles that had to be overcome to close the highway. He stated that it would be impossible and that local opposition might be fierce. We were however undaunted by his pessimism.

I was directed to develop a plan for the new building, the layout and estimate the cost. We knew we had a very difficult task ahead of us. We developed blueprints for the building but I suggested that we create an interior model of the building and three-dimensional pictures of how the building would look when finished. We put together a presentation of the building in a small folding three ring binder. We contacted the state governor and office of business development to engender more support. The business development office was enthusiastic. Next, we built the interior model of the building to scale and put it on a large table in a large conference room. Then we invited our own employees to visit the conference room with the scale model, play with the layout and make suggestions. We received many helpful suggestions that we immediately deployed in the model and the building plans.

We then personally visited each house along the route that the highway was going to be diverted to and explained the concept and what the building was going to look like. We invited them to take a personal tour of the plant and most of them toured the plant. There were no objections from the home owners. Within a month the state business development office informed us that closing the highway had been approved by the state transportation department. Our next step was to get approval from corporate for capital funds. Capital money was tight that year, so we created a plan that only showed half the building and its layout. We did bring the plan of the whole building with us and the cost estimates.

The capital committee was so impressed with the building layout and the work that we had done that they asked to see the layout of the entire building. They approved the money for the entire building. Yes, we did invite the state representative who said it would be impossible to reroute the state highway to the ribbon cutting ceremony. Leadership is the art of accomplishing the impossible so what if no one Has ever done it before.

Share Your Hard Lessons Learned With Others Do Not Embellish Them.

The production scheduler of a large Paper Mill was forced to retire and was downsized. He had been there for over thirty years. Much to my surprise and chagrin, I was forced to take his place. It was a large integrated paper mill with over 2000 employees and over 3000 different SKUs or brands. There were over 200 constraints and, in a scheduling, meeting the biggest bully usually got their way. I had industrial engineering experience but no experience in process industry scheduling. Worst, the retiring scheduler refused to help or train me. He did the entire scheduling by hand using long green sheets on his desk. All his knowledge was locked in his head and he refused to release it.

The job was a great responsibility, and downtime in a Paper Mill was tabulated by accounting, as being worth over $100,000 an hour negative impact to the budget. My boss got me a personal computer, the first in the plant, and I proceeded to put the production schedule on Lotus 123 file spreadsheets. I would print out the files and they sort of imitated the long green sheets. I would glue them together on the wall of the office. I was so nervous that I actually scheduled an entire year's worth of production, and hung up all the spreadsheets on the office wall. This project took me over a hundred hours. I did not stop until it was done.

After all this work, I was in my office late one evening staring at the hung-up production spreadsheets and had an "ah ha" moment. There was a pattern to the schedule for each quarter. The pattern roughly repeated itself for every quarter in the year. In other words, the schedule remained very similar for each quarter.

I decided to look up information on process industry scheduling. In one journal article I stumbled upon a concept called cycle scheduling. Basically, the concept establishes an optimal production cycle for the plant or mill. If the scheduler is forced to break the cycle for an extraordinary reason, the scheduler tries to get back to the cycle or pattern as soon as possible. The pattern or cycle remains approximately the same when in place.

I was ecstatic, now I was using a best practice for process industry production scheduling. I soon expanded my production schedule and built an in house MRP (Material Requirements Planning) system which really improved material flow.

At a corporate meeting of production schedulers, I shared my findings with all the other schedulers and explained the concept of cycle scheduling. I made sure that they also knew that it was an industry best practice and not something that I had invented on my own. I made it clear that it was optional for them to use cycle scheduling and not a requirement. They understood the large amount of work that I had done and were very appreciative of my sharing it with them. I then helped many of them set it up for their plants. Share your hard lessons learned with others do not embellish them.

Be Humble But Be Confident

The CEO of our company came to our plant to give us an award for safety plant of the year. This was the most prestigious company award and safety was the highest priority. I was in the human resources department at the time. The plant manager accepted the award and asked me to say a few words since I had led the plant safety team. I accepted the award but called out each member of the safety team to come up front to the stage. I gave them the credit for achieving the award and praised their hard work and dedication. I closed with saying that we would do our best to win the award next year. The CEO insisted on taking a picture with the entire team. Be humble but be confident.

Praise People Who Do A Good Job Often

I ran a team of eight employees who did supply chain functions. When one of them did an outstanding job, I would reward them with some time off for the accomplishment. This time off reward seems to be the most popular with the team. I decided to expand the praise. I had a background in football coaching and we would put stickers on a player's helmet when they made a good play. Since we did not wear helmets, I constructed a bulletin board with each individuals name on it. Whenever they did very well, I would put a sticker next to their name and run the stickers horizontally across the board. The prize for ten stickers was me buying them lunch. They all relished in the fact that I had to buy them lunch. I did limit the lunch to a particular local restaurant, but the banter by the whole team as a person was getting closer to a free lunch, was particularly rambunctious and funny. Praise people who do a good job often.

Treat People Like You Would Like To Be Treated.

Late one Friday afternoon I was working late in my Human Resources office. My phone rang and I identified myself and my title. The person on the other end of the line sounded frantic and wanted to order some cases of our products. I informed them that this was Human Resources and not Distribution but she pleaded for me to please help. She proceeded to list her order and what she needed. It was a list of about 15 of our most popular brands. I wrote it down and repeated the request back to her. I also gave her our fax number in Human Resources and requested that she fax the order to me. I would wait and let her know if I received the fax. I told her that I would put the phone down and go to the fax machine. I stood by the fax machine and sure enough, the fax shortly came through with the brands she ordered and where to ship it. I requested her phone number and said I would call her back shortly.

I quickly walked over to the distribution center and talked directly to the shipping manager. I showed him the order and he recognized the person who requested the order. He put the order together immediately and procured a truck to rush ship it to the requested location. I then went back to my office and called her back and gave her the order number. She thanked me profusely. Subsequently the order arrived that night to the required location.

After the weekend, I learned that the order was shipped directly to a marketing and trade show of one of our major customers that showcased our product. Treat people like you would like to be treated.

Leaders Work Hard And Volunteer For The Tough Assignments.

I was working for a fortune 500 company as an employee relations manager, in human resources, in a large midwestern plant. The company had just undergone a very tough period. It had gone to war with its employees and tried to break the current union and implemented a take it or leave it contract. All this did was infuriate the employees and create a giant slowdown in the plant. Fortunately, the company decided to reverse this approach and work with the union and employees as a partner. One of the goals was to reduce the number of skilled trades in the plant from the current 29 classifications. This created much inefficiency and complicated rules. It literally could take three people to change a lightbulb.

The company hired a consultant in creating partnerships and improving employee relationships for three days. The fee was over $10,000 for the sessions. I sat in on the sessions. I soon realized that I was much more knowledgeable about our union, the culture, the skilled trades and the approach that we needed to implement pay-for-skill than the consultant. I decided to do research on my own and discovered some articles on pay-for-skill and skilled trade consolidation. After a discussion with my boss I volunteered to lead the skilled trades consolidation and implement a pay-for skill compensation system. This was a tough and contentious project. I was to be the first in the company to lead the implementation of the compensation system.

Despite the company's attempts to destroy the union, the union president and the union committee still trusted me, and considered me fair and open to compromise. I decided to become an expert on pay-for- skill compensation and started researching the concept. I had always considered getting a PhD, and now I investigated options for a PhD, and made a dissertation proposal to a university. I would research organizations that already had similar pay-for-skills systems and study the factors that made them successful.

They accepted the proposal. My logic was since I had to do the research anyway for my work-life, why not jointly take an academic approach to pay-for-skill. I received help from the local university in my research and the use of a super-computer to analyze my data. After working long and hard with the union, we jointly reduced the skilled trade classifications from 29 to 5. Crafts persons could also become multi-skilled and have multiple skills such as welder pipe-fitter and carpenter combined! The more skills, the higher pay they received. Crafts persons were not pressured to have multiple skills, but if they did not, their pay would not be as much as a crafts person with multiple skills. Their skills training was subsidized by the company and we established an on-site tech-school for them to gain the skills. We also extended the opportunity for skills training to production workers and management.

I finished the PhD in four years and published the results of my data. The overall knowledge and understanding of the workforce improved dramatically. Pay-for-skill is a long-term investment in employees that is exceptionally successful. The project gave me a reputation for volunteering for tough assignments. Leaders work hard and volunteer for the tough assignments.

Be Pleasant Positive And Polite

I have extensive functional procurement and supply management experience. This attribute attracted an e-procurement software company to hire me as a sales representative and software installer. I went through a rigorous software boot camp and went to my first installation client. I was obviously very nervous and wanted to make sure that the client was satisfied with my performance and that the software installation went well.

The client was a software company also but not in supply management. This was the equivalent of installing plumbing in a plumber's house! They were highly critical of the capabilities of our e-procurement software and its limitations. I soon had a long punch list of aspects of our software that they were not satisfied with or wanted improved. Despite many of the people being sarcastic, belligerent and disruptive I remained positive and polite. Being new to the company I diligently sent every one of their requests up the chain to corporate development. I also made sure by phone call that development completely understood their requests.

The night before go-live day I received the software installation disks from corporate. Much to my surprise the installation disks were version 6.0 and the client had only paid for version 5.0, I could not get anyone to give me any direction on what to do, and with the deadline fast approaching, I decided to install version 6.0. As I went through the testing, I was relieved that the new software was up and running and stable. It had passed all the benchmark tests. I however, was not looking forward to the meeting with the client the next day. I was sure that they would find even more issues that they wanted improved and would be impolite and nasty to me.

I started the meeting and before I could get into the training plan, one of my client's harshest critics spoke up, "Mr.

DePaoli I want to commend you and I apologize to you. You have maintained your positive attitude despite our criticisms. I signed onto the software very early this morning and checked all the punch list issues that we had talked about and they were fixed. I apologize for being so critical of you and your company." Although I was more shocked than him about these circumstances, I remained composed and just replied, "Great! I stayed up all night modifying the software to solve those issues and your punch list." What was amazing was that I said it convincingly and with a straight face.

What had happened was that I, like a good soldier had sent all these issues to development using the system required, and they had incorporated them directly into version 6.0 as a fix or as an option. Our client was ecstatic and within three months the client requested to upgrade to version 7.0. They specifically asked for me to personally install it. Luckily, I was already involved in another major project and our vice president of sales assigned another installer to them that he said that I specifically recommended for them. They remained loyal customers for many years. Always be pleasant, positive and polite.

Always Do Your Best Even For The Tasks That You Hate To Do.

I was the leader of a team that had to do inventory cycle counts ever month. The computer would type out a list of parts to be actually found and counted. We usually did the counts on Saturday because the plant was less active. The goal is 95% accuracy or verifications. Many of the parts were scattered around the plant is dirty or hard to get areas. As a team we divided up the tasks and went out and verified the part count. We then met back as a group and the parts that had erroneous counts, required us to get another person to verify the actual count. We then had to input the actual counts into the inventory database. There was no glamor in this task but it was very necessary to ensure our production planning had the right starting point for production runs. We prided ourselves in the fact that we exceeded the 95% accuracy in the verifications. Always Do Your best even for the tasks that you hate to do.

Take An Interest In People, Not Toys, Technology Or Hardware.

LET ME TAKE OVER FOR AWHILE SO YOU CAN TAKE A BREAK . . .

I was selected to be the Team Manager (supervisor) for the introduction of a new major consumer product. I was very nervous about understanding the technology, computer reports and production hardware. Luckily, I was with the installation engineers and learned a lot about the technology and they taught me how to actually run the high-speed machines. There was a lot of pressure to roll out the new product before the competition. We were working seven days a week non-stop. I had no problems with the technology, computer programs or new add-ons to the production equipment, but was struggling to get the trust and confidence from my team. Third or night shift was particularly hard on all of us and around early morning hours you could see some members of my crew struggling to stay awake. So, I decided to take action. When I saw a team member nearly nodding off, I went up to them and told them to take a 15-minute break and I took over running the machine myself. When they came back, they resumed the machine operation. I did this as often as feasible and tried not to favor any employees. The risk I took was having an accident and getting hurt, but I was well trained.

After these break relief actions, my crew members opened up to me in conversations and machine problems. I was invited to card games during the lunch period and joined in on their banter. Their trust in me grew. Take an interest in people, not toys, technology or hardware

ABOUT THE AUTHOR

Dr. Tom DePaoli, (Dr. Tom) is currently an independent management consultant, the Principal of Apollo Solutions (http://www.apollosolutions.us), which does general business consulting in the human resources, supply chain and lean six sigma areas. He founded his organization in 1995. Recently, he retired as a Captain from the Navy Reserve after over 30 years of service. In other civilian careers, Dr. Tom was a supply chain and human resources executive with corporate purchasing turnaround experience and lean six sigma deployments. He has worked for over ten major companies and consulted for over fifty organizations throughout his career. Some of his consulting projects included: information systems projects, re-engineering organizations, transformation, e-procurement, e-commerce, change management, global sourcing and negotiating. His industry experience is in the chemical, paper, pharmaceutical, Information technology, automotive, government, consumer, equipment, services and consulting businesses. He has been published extensively in journals, magazines and books. He has been involved in many forms of communications including website design, marketing campaigns, political campaigns, radio advertisements, and scripts. He is the author

of ten books. His Amazon author's page is
https://www.amazon.com/author/tomdepaoli

He has instructed at six education facilities in
numerous roles. He is active in supporting the
YMCA, Wounded Warrior, and the prevention of
the bullying of children. For more detailed
information about Dr. Tom see his LinkedIn
homepage.

https://www.linkedin.com/in/drtomdepaoli/

Summaries of the Author's Other Books All Available on Amazon.com

Common Sense Purchasing

Common Sense Purchasing is a no-holds-barred practical guide to purchasing, relationships and negotiations success. If you don't like consultants, buzzwords and theory, then this non-traditional book is meant for you. Straight forward and to the point, this book will be difficult to put down until you have finished the supply chain journey. Dr. Tom DePaoli, a veteran purchasing pro, learned his purchasing lessons the hard way and wants to share his valuable insights for purchasing people and all business professionals. Common Sense Purchasing reveals the real-life lessons learned from a purchasing

professional who has seen every purchasing job level from junior buyer to vice president.

Purchasing is the art of relationships and trust building that requires deft handling. Dr. Tom DePaoli has led numerous efforts to reengineer purchasing and has successfully negotiated international supply agreements. He provides poignant insights into what really works in purchasing and separates the theory that doesn't work from the practical aspects that were very successful in his career. Dr. Tom uses many of his original sayings and hard knock lessons to help purchasing professionals get it right. Purchasing is the art of building relationships. It is not about negotiations, transactions, industry knowledge, market knowledge, know-how or technology. It is all about building strong relationships and gaining the trust of suppliers, customers, and colleagues.

Nothing else even comes close in importance for successful purchasing as does the creation of strong relationships. Just an outstanding purchasing field manual! Most consultants and academic folks will hate this book! They can't stand low-cost common-sense techniques. The book has many simple common-sense approaches to purchasing. Unfortunately, common sense is all too rare in purchasing.

At our company we don't even want to hire purchasing folks who are certified. We have to spend too much time deprogramming them! The style is eclectic because the author wanted to emulate the chaos of a typical purchasing day. Many bureaucrats can't get this book and just mindlessly pan it. The key point is that relationship building with suppliers is essential. There is no roadmap for this effort other than hard work and getting folks to trust each other. Strategists like Dr. Tom are rare but their gains can be enormous. Dr. Tom is a true and dynamic strategic thinker whose ideas are timeless and right on. Buy this book and use it. Make everyone in your department read it and discuss it. (Book review excerpts about the book)

Common Sense Supply Management

In his new guide to supply management, author Thomas DePaoli offers no-nonsense strategies learned from his diverse career in many organizations. Told in part via a story format, Common Sense Supply Management uses real life examples to discuss what goes right, and often wrong, in the supply chain management trenches. The stories are told factually without any embellishing notes to distract the reader.

By carefully following this book's accounts, supply management professionals can learn a career's worth of what to do and what not to do. DePaoli provides practical lessons launched from real-life cases and tested in the unforgiving supply chain management reality.

Like many good business leaders, the author places business relationships first and foremost in his guide. "Supply management covers more breadth and depth than any other discipline in an organization," says DePaoli. "It is the art of building multiple relationships."

His book advances to tackle best practices, Lean Six Sigma, and information-based negotiations. He includes an extensive chapter on planning and strategy that prepares the reader for his multi-dimensional approach to suppliers, offering proven tactics for testing and sourcing suppliers, and he is candid about the possible pitfalls of using international sourcing. A stickler for robust, data-driven decisions, he shows the sorts of metrics supply managers should be tracking. He discusses a range of computer-based tools that allow professionals to conduct their business. He warns managers about adopting slick-looking technologies that remain incompatible with an organization's culture. He remains convinced that his story-telling strategy will allow readers to learn more than what any textbook offers. "Some of the stories are good management lessons," says DePaoli. "Others were the result of having great people work for me and teamwork, while others were the result of just hard work and massive amounts of tough homework."

Supply chain management continues to form the backbone of most companies. Knowing how to orchestrate its complexity can give an organization a strong competitive edge. The supply managers who are willing to take the journey and possess the indomitable spirit necessary to succeed will greatly benefit from this unorthodox but powerful guide.

Growing up Italian in the Fifties or How Most of Us Became Good Wise Guys

In the grand scheme of things, sixty years is not a very long time. With the explosion of technology, however, that amount of time encompasses seismic shifts in the American cultural landscape. The 1950's in the United States were a much simpler, more naive time than what it is today. And in the big and small cities alike, neighborhoods were ethnically defined: Italian, Irish, Polish, etc. This ingrained a deep sense of pride in ancestry and the close-knit feeling of extended families.

Highlighting the importance of family and the feeling inspired by his large, loving Italian brood, Tom DePaoli captures the experiences of growing up in a different era and its effects on those fortunate enough to have grown up in it. Today children are surrounded by video games, iPods, and personal computers, devices that remove them from the world and isolate them from friends and family.

For the author, his family, and his friends, the only gadget they really had was their enthusiasm for sports and the limitless terrain of their imagination. Playing baseball in little league, football and baseball in the sandlot, and escaping to the nearby woods for adventure, they relied on experiencing life with one another rather than doing so alone through modern technology. Including colorful depictions of his mother, father, Uncle Pat, Aunt Bert, and a list of family that seems endless, this collection of short reminiscences boils over with the feelings of loyalty, closeness, and love borne of a generation whose values are seemingly lost in the never-ending march of technological progress.

Tom DePaoli's vivid picture of his extended Italian family is a homage to a bygone era when brothers, sisters, aunts, uncles, grandparents, everyone lived in the same neighborhood and were indeed a village raising the children. Engrossing and full of life, Growing Up Italian in the 50's is an ode to a time that was, indeed, the "Good Old Days".

This heartwarming read will take you back to an era, when you weren't obsessed with electronics and used your imagination to entertain yourself. Several of the Author's stories and photos took me back to my Midwestern small town as a child and I can relate to many of his wonderful writings. Grab a glass of Iced Tea and enjoy reading about the sense of community, family values, and how sports played an important role in many of the childhood memories during the 50's. I grew up in the 60's, but so much reminds me of my daily visits at my Grandparents home. I also enjoyed visiting the "neighbors" with my Mom for tea frequently. I miss those days! "We all had parents who were strict but cared about us."

Jayson and the Corporate Argonauts – the Quest for the Golden Fleece of Transformation

In his guide to organizational transformation, author Tom DePaoli simplifies the strategies learned from his diverse career in many organizations. The book does an analogy of the Greek tale of Jason and the Argonauts Quest for the

Golden Fleece. In this new tale, Jayson and the Corporate Argonauts - the Quest for the Golden Fleece of Transformation DePaoli suggests strategies for transforming an organization.

The book follows the adventures of the Greek hero Jason and his Argonauts and draws on the lessons learned from the crew and the perils that they overcome. The reader should try to become familiar with the Greek myth which the book explains. These adventures are used to recommend strategies for modern Corporate Argonauts trying to transform their organization. The quest for organizational transformation is a more perilous journey than the Greek quest for the Golden Fleece.

Many organizations do not have any experience in this dynamic process and falter. The book remains true to the myth of Jason's journey and the need for organizations to constantly transform. DePaoli provides practical lessons learned from his real-life cases of transformation, tested in harsh competitive reality. The emphasis is on the key concepts that can make transformation successful. Since every organization is different the author concentrates on the important strategic principles not the tactical methodology.

The reader does not have to be familiar with the Greek tale, but the author does recommend at least becoming acquainted with a summary of the adventures. The author makes the adventures relevant to dealing with change and organizational transformation. DePaoli kept the methods simple and to the point. The fun is in the quest or the journey. He reveals the right methods that can help avoid the missteps of change and transformation. The author admits that there were many failures in his career especially when attempting to have people not only accept change but proselytize change. Organizations need both compassion and integrity to succeed. Corporate Argonauts should be given the chance to join the crew of the Argo and begin transformation.

Kaizen Kreativity (OOPS!)

In his new fun and creative book Kaizen Kreativity (Oops) or Don't Be Afraid of Looking Stupid. I'm an Expert at It! author Dr. Tom DePaoli offers an entertaining and creative approach to improving work design and work processes. Dr. DePaoli uses a variety of techniques including storytelling, imaginative training exercises and ready to go outlines of Power Points on Kaizens.

Dr. DePaoli uses self-deprecating humor to recall the many times when he stumbled, when trying to implement Kaizen events. The reader can gain much from these lessons.

The book also serves as a good desktop guide to Kaizens with a wealth of information on how to organize for Kaizen events. This is not a dogmatic book that insists on a rigid methodology for Kaizens. Dr. DePaoli often shows that just using a few Kaizen tools can often result in significant gains. The book will help both the novice and the experienced Kaizen leader. He uses real life examples of Kaizen tools to show how work groups can make great gains. By following these stories, the reader can gain a career's worth of experience in Kaizen events. Dr. DePaoli's lessons are practical, to the point and enjoyable.

Like many good business leaders, the author places getting the trust of the Kaizen work team first and foremost in his book. He emphasizes the intense preparations for the Kaizen event and overcoming the fear of asking stupid questions and conquering any trepidation of looking foolish. His book advances to tackle common mistakes in the Kaizen event, dealing with Kaizen team bad actors and building a strong relationship with the

Kaizen champion. He provides an excellent workbook outline for a Kaizen event along with a strong glossary of Kaizen terms. The book provides solid elements of a desktop guide for conducting a Kaizen along with suggestions on how to make the Kaizen tools exciting. This is novel indispensable guide to a Kaizen event. Dr. DePaoli asserts, "Above all don't be afraid of looking stupid! I'm an expert at it! And it has served me very well."

Sydney the Monster Stops Bullies

"The story's bottom line is a powerful moral of friendship, love and support; forces that can transcend bullying and bring any child's life back on track," explains the author. "It is vital that children learn to recognize the social, physical and psychological effect that are part and parcel of bullying. Preaching directly to children doesn't work, so I opted for an enchanting story with a happy ending! All kids love monsters, hence why I created such an unusual main character. Sydney is able to influence children in a way no human can, and the fact that he is one step removed from real life allows children to confide in his message in a way they simply couldn't with any friend or relative. It's powerful stuff."

The author sees wide appeal for his work. "There's no denying that bullying is an epidemic that knows no geographical or cultural boundaries. Therefore, this book has truly global potential. There should be a copy in in every home, school, church or any place where young people congregate. It contains a message they desperately need to hear." 'Sydney the Monster Stops Bullies' is available now!

In Dr. Tom DePaoli's 'Sydney the Monster Stops Bullies', a quirky and friendly monster overcomes his own bullying nightmare to emerge a true victorious hero. Through a story that is entertaining, uplifting yet inherently serious, young readers will not only learn how to spot bullying and its social, physical and mental detriments – but also find the empowerment they need to respect humanity's rich differences.

'Sydney the Monster Stops Bullies' is the latest release from Dr. Tom DePaoli. The volume's premise is bold and clear-cut: to teach children what bullying really is, how it can plight their lives and what they can do to help friends who may be suffering. Oh yes, it will also make them more tolerant, too! Synopsis: Sydney the Monster Stops Bullies is about Sydney the monster who is a friendly monster and uses special monster powers to stop bullies and teach children to respect differences. Sydney is a first bullied by the other monsters but then becomes a hero! "The story's bottom line is a powerful moral of friendship, love and support; forces that can transcend bullying and bring any child's life back on track," explains the author. "It is vital that children learn to recognize the social, physical and psychological effect that are part and parcel of bullying. Preaching directly to children doesn't work, so I opted for an enchanting story with a happy ending! All kids love monsters, hence why I created such an unusual main character. Sydney is able to influence children in a way no human can, and the fact that he is one step removed from real life allows children to confide in his message in a way they simply couldn't with any friend or relative. It's powerful stuff." The author sees wide appeal for his work.

"There's no denying that bullying is an epidemic that knows no geographical or cultural boundaries. Therefore, this book has truly global potential. There should be a copy in in every home, school, church or any place where young people congregate. It contains a message they desperately need to hear." '

Sydney the Monster Stops Cyber Bullies

Sydney the Monster Stops Cyber Bullies is a new approach children's book. Dr. Tom DePaoli offers practical strategies and tactics, for parents, children, teachers, and relatives to prevent cyber bullying. The book is written for both adults and children on the increasingly prevalent and hurtful subject of cyber bullying.

Dr. Tom challenges all readers to become committed to preventing cyber bullying. He reveals many suggestions to prevent cyber bulling. He recommends policies and organizations to help when cyber bullying occurs. This book is a very good source book on cyber bullying and an exceptional introduction to children on this controversial topic. Dr. Tom recommends that parents read the book aloud to their children, extemporize when necessary, and build their knowledge base on how to prevent children from being cyber bullied.

This is a serious and troubling topic. Dr. Tom offers outstanding preventive and corrective measures. He uses his well-known Sydney the Monster character to make children aware of cyber bulling. The book serves as a landmark guide for eradicating cyber bullying.

Avoiding a Supply Chain Apocalypse

Purchasing and supply chain professionals don't abandon ship! Here is an alternative approach to becoming a Supply Chain Doomsday Prepper for a Supply Chain Apocalypse! In his creative guide Avoiding a Supply Chain Apocalypse – the Best of Dr. Tom, Dr. Tom DePaoli offers practical strategies and tactics, learned and tested from his purchasing and supply chain career.

He does not recommend a single silver bullet or quick fix, but suggests a multi-faceted diverse approach to avoiding supply chain meltdowns. Dr. DePaoli challenges the reader to survey his best writings and to select what fits their particular organizational cultures. There is no one size fits all in the supply chain. As the importance of supply chain management grows leaps and bounds; the supply chain professional must develop multiple options and proficient tactics to insure the continuity of the supply chain.

Of particular importance is "Purchasing is the art of building relationships. It is not about negotiations, transactions, industry knowledge, market knowledge, know-how or technology. It is all about building strong relationships and gaining the trust of suppliers, customers, and colleagues.

There is no easy way to get employees to trust you. One of things that I've always done is to make sure that I do what I told them I was going to do. Nothing impresses employees more than keeping your word. Another good tactic to use is to always admit your mistakes and do not try to cover them up. Employees appreciate when you invest the time and effort to train them. Make sure you have a training plan for all of your employees. Try to behave ethically, employees expect you to lead by example and to live by your word. Communicate to them daily if possible, in use as many different channels of communication as you can."

"The fact is that purchasing also runs its own Research and Development (R&D) department. Suppliers, in collaboration with purchasing, are perhaps the most cost-effective R&D function in a company. Jointly they often come up with leaps in technology and transformations in products. When they cooperate, they can transform a company and its products. Breakthroughs that occur via this method should receive as much publicity if not more than those developed internally! In summary getting purchasing valued for its great contribution to revenue; requires both a bottom-up and top-down approach. Empower as many employees as possible to participate in purchasing and solicit their ideas and suggestions. Set up one-on-one executive exchanges with your supplier executives. Finally, systematically create a strong marketing plan to communicate your successes." The book serves as a guide for the purchasing or supply chain professional to optimize their supply chain and avoid disaster.

Broken Windows Management for Business

In his creative guide to the practice of Broken Windows Management for Business, author Dr. Tom DePaoli offers practical strategies learned from his diverse career in many organizations. A description of some of the principles of broken windows management is explained and made relevant to both business and other organizations.

The broken windows management analogy to some criminal justice theories can be explained. In many cities of the country there's a fear of the streets especially if there's disorder and the environment is in disarray. In many organizations there's a fear of management. No small part of this can be due to employees who do not understand the actions of upper management. One of Deming's most important points was to drive out fear. Prevention of disorder and actually fixing things that employees say are wrong; goes a very long way in establishing trust and credibility with management. Management must be vigilant and constantly try to control disorder and fix the things and issues that employees' value.

These actions reduce employee fear of management and actually help gain trust. Trust is enhanced by quickly fixing things that employees' want fixed. The author relates some for the principles of 5S and the kaizen methodology to the broken windows management approach.

Told in part via a story or blog post like format, Broken Windows Management for Business uses real life examples to discuss what goes right, and often wrong, in the broken windows management trenches. Dr. Tom contrasts the broken windows management approach to current management fads, which are often ineffective, trendy, and shallow flavors-of-the-month.

Broken Windows Management is a strong action and results orientated approach, which requires a powerful ongoing commitment from management. The emphasis is on fixing employee issues, correcting complaints and solving problems expeditiously. Attention to detail and a passion for meeting employee's needs are at its centerpiece. Broken Windows

Management also places an emphasis on order and trying to create an impressive workplace than employees and customers would be proud of and motivated to keep clean. Dr. DePaoli sets a benchmark that the work area should be so impressive and safe that employees could take-their-child-to-work any day, at any time. Like some good business leaders (unfortunately now in the minority), the author places employee needs first and foremost in his book.

"Many organizations have lost sight of the value of their employees and treat them very poorly. They can provide an energized face to the customer that will provide a significant competitive advantage."

The actual theory of broken windows management for business is not complicated. It does not require tedious certifications; long training sessions or expensive consultants. It does require a strong commitment from management to listen to employee complaints, get well organized and fix them.

Another benefit of using broken windows management for business is that it builds everyone's skills in maintenance, problem solving and creative approaches workplace design. The theories of clean design and ergonomics can also help. Dr. DePaoli remains convinced that broken windows management for business is a proven and effective method to improve employee trust and loyalty. A lot of broken windows management is learning by doing. There is ample room for creativity and having fun with broken windows management. I wish you well in your broken windows management journey. I for one know that it works, and I am sure that you will develop a faith in broken windows management, it is one of the most viable and practical ways to achieve quality of work life improvement.

Broken windows management is not a silver bullet or a theory that will fix all the problems in an organization. It is certainly something to consider based on the failure of many other management flavor-of-the-month attempts to improve employee morale.

Finally, if you give employees the tools and resources to fix many of the issues and problems on their own, without interference from upper management, you will establish a strong culture of self-reliance and skills for employees to solve their own issues. Broken windows management greatly encourages solving issues at the lowest or core level, a fundamentally strong management principle. Giving broken windows

management a chance can empower
employees and improve management
credibility tremendously.

Boogeyman Leadership: How to Turn Your Employees into Listless Zombies

Don't let the title scare you! The bad
leaders will. Dr. Tom DePaoli in Boogeyman
Leadership: How to Turn Your Employees
into Listless Zombies, showcases poor
leaders and their tactics that inevitably fail.
He believes you should know what does
not work first, so that an aspiring good
leader does not waste time on such failed
approaches. He does not pretend to offer
any silver bullet solutions to correct these
poor leadership policies.

He defines boogeyman leadership as the
use of miserable and intimidating
leadership tactics whose purpose is to
terrify employees and instill distrust,
apathy and fear. The result is a zombie-like
listless state.

Boogeyman Leadership recounts many bad
leadership ideas and real-life stories to
make sure the reader crosses these
schemes off their leadership list. The reader
should be forewarned that many of the bad
leadership ideas are repetitive. Bad leaders
are not very creative! The book is

not a solemn academic book or a guide to great leadership successes. Its purpose is to give examples of terrible leadership and worse management tactics that Dr. Tom and others have experienced in their careers.

Dr. Tom suggests the reader re-visualize their own personal leaders, that they have had, who have used the very same or similar defective devices. Dr. Tom sadly notes that these failed leadership ploys are becoming even more common, destructive and hurtful. He urges the reader to avoid these methods at all costs. Followers never forget bullying leaders.

ABOUT THE ILLUSTRATOR

MISSION STATEMENT:
"Making the World A Happier Place, One Smile at a Time."TM

"Art should be fun!" states illustrator/artist Laurie Barrows.
The artist's work sparkles with playfulness.
Her positive approach to life shines through.
Bright color celebrates the joy the artist finds in her subject.
This is her 233 book.

"Success has many definitions. If my work makes you smile,
and brightens your day, I've been successful."

www.LaurieBarrows.com

lauriebarrows@att.net

NOTES & IDEAS

NOTES & IDEAS

NOTES & IDEAS

NOTES & IDEAS

NOTES & IDEAS

NOTES & IDEAS

NOTES & IDEAS

NOTES & IDEAS

NOTES & IDEAS

NOTES & IDEAS

Made in the USA
Coppell, TX
29 June 2020